To Zuniyah and Judah from Suzy

STERLING CHILDREN'S BOOKS
New York

An Imprint of Sterling Publishing Co., Inc.
1166 Avenue of the Americas
New York, NY 10036

ISBN 978-1-4549-3205-5

Distributed in Canada by Sterling Publishing Co., Inc.
c/o Canadian Manda Group, 664 Annette Street
Toronto, Ontario M6S 2C8, Canada
Distributed in the United Kingdom by GMC Distribution Services
Castle Place, 166 High Street, Lewes, East Sussex BN7 1XU, England
Distributed in Australia by NewSouth Books
45 Beach Street, Coogee, NSW 2034, Australia

For information about custom editions, special sales, and premium and corporate purchases,
please contact Sterling Special Sales at 800-805-5489 or specialsales@sterlingpublishing.com.

Manufactured in China

Lot #:
2 4 6 8 10 9 7 5 3 1
10/18

sterlingpublishing.com

PHOTOGRAPHS: Alamy: The History Collection: 2 inset (2)
iStock: amysuem: i; AnthiaCumming: 4 middle; D4Fish: 3, 4 bottom; Steve Debenport: 6;
FatCamera: 9, 19, 24, back cover top; Fertnig: 20; fotokostic: 1; kali9: 23; Lorado: 14; VPH
Photography: 5 right; xjben: 21; Yobro10: 14
Shutterstock: ESB Professional: 4 top; Fotokostic: cover, 13, 18, back cover bottom; MaZiKab: 5 left;
UKRID: 2 background, 4 background, 16

LET'S PLAY

SOCCER

*Everything You Need to Know
for Your First Practice*

By Susan Blackaby

STERLING CHILDREN'S BOOKS
New York

History

Soccer is a fast, fun game. It has been kicking around for more than 2,000 years! When it started in China, it was called football. The game soon spread all around the world. In the 1800s, players in England set up a group of teams. They named the group Association Football. They called it "soccer" for short. The name stuck in the United States. In most other places, soccer is still called football.

GLOSSARY

Here are some soccer words to know. Watch for them as you read.

Attacker—The player who tries to score.

Cleats—Soccer shoes.

Defender—The player who tries to keep the other team from scoring.

Dribbling—Moving the ball with your feet.

Forward (striker)—Main attacker on a team.

Goal—Space the ball passes through in order to score.

Jersey—Soccer shirt.

Midfielder—Player who backs up the striker.

Pass—Sending the ball to another player on your team.

Pitch—The soccer field.

Shin guards—The pads for your lower legs.

Trap—Stopping the ball with your foot.

The Gear

You do not need a lot of gear to play soccer. You need a ball. You need some pals. You need a **pitch**, which is a place to play. You need to know where to kick the ball in order to score. Soccer nets work best to mark each **goal**. But you can use cones, or any other marker you want! A couple of sweatshirts do just fine in a pinch.

If you play on a team, you will need some extra gear.

Outdoor soccer shoes are called **cleats**. Cleats are shoes with studs on the soles. The studs help you keep your grip on grass.

Shin guards are pads to wear on your legs. When you play, your legs can get hit by the ball or accidentally kicked by a player. Shin guards help keep you from getting hurt.

When you play on a team, shin guards are a must. You will wear them under your soccer socks. Shorts and a shirt called a **jersey** are also part of your soccer uniform. Players on each team wear jerseys that are alike. They make your teammates easy to spot.

Are You Ready to Play?

Here are the things you need to know to be a soccer star.

The first rule of soccer is *no hands*! Soccer is a game for feet!

If the ball bounces out of bounds, you will use both hands to throw the ball onto the field. Otherwise, you will use only your feet.

Older players and pros can bounce the ball off their heads. "Heading the ball" may be hard on your neck and bad for your brain. Soccer rules say you have to wait four or five more years before you try it in practices or games.

Dribbling

Dribbling is moving the ball with your feet while you run. You will dribble the ball up and down the field. But you can practice dribbling even if you are standing still. Use the inside of your foot. Tap the ball from foot to foot.

When you have room to move, start out by walking. Use the inside of your foot. Tap the ball from foot to foot with each step. Try to keep the ball close to your feet and under control.

Little by little, you can speed up. Start with a fast walk and keep the ball just ahead of you. Work up to a jog, but don't let the ball get away from you. On a run, you can kick the ball ahead of you a little ways. Then run to catch up with it.

As you get better, you will practice dribbling with different parts of your feet to switch direction as you move. You might also find out you have one foot that is stronger than the other. Give your weak foot more practice.

You should also practice keeping your head up. Learning to dribble without watching your feet is an important skill!

In a game, you will keep the ball in close to you if the kids on the other team are nearby. That way it will be harder for them to steal it away from you. If the field is wide open, you can kick the ball farther in front of you.

Passing

Using your feet to hang onto the ball is a key skill. Using your feet to get rid of the ball is important, too!

Kids on the other team will try to get the ball away from you. Before that can happen, try to **pass** the ball to one of your teammates. When you pass the ball, you stop dribbling. You plant one foot so that it is aimed at the player receiving the pass. Kick the ball with your other foot. Follow through by moving your kicking leg toward your target. This action helps your kick land where you want it to go.

You can use different parts of your foot for different kinds of passes, but try to keep the ball bouncing low on the ground. For a short pass, you can kick the ball using the inside of your foot.

To receive a pass, you **trap** the ball with your foot to make it stop rolling. To do this, first plant one foot firmly on the ground. Then, use your other foot to step on the ball or stop it with the side of your foot. Then you can dribble it up the field. In the meantime, your teammates will be getting into position so you can pass the ball to them.

Your coach will have you do *a lot* of passing drills. Get together with a pal and practice, practice, practice.

Scoring

When your team has the ball, players work together to try to score. You run the ball up the field, dribbling and passing. Your team scores a **goal** when a player kicks the ball into the net or between the cones.

Older kids and pro teams have a player called a goalie. The goalie's job is to block shots so the other team doesn't score. Goalies are the only players who can touch the ball with their hands.

You can practice scoring goals any time. You want to be able to kick the ball so that it goes exactly where you want it to. When you practice, aim at a target. Kick the ball using different parts of your foot. Kick the ball from all different angles. Kicks off the top of your foot lift the ball up in a high arc. Toe kicks can wobble off track.

Who Is on the Pitch?

Big kids and pros use 11 players on each team. They need that many because they play on a huge pitch. They need to cover a lot of ground! Plus they have a goalie. They play two 45-minute halves. If a game is tied, it goes into overtime.

You will play on a smaller pitch with three or four kids on a team. Subs sit on the bench. Each game has four 12-minute quarters and a 5-minute halftime. Everyone will get a chance to play. If the game is tied at the end, everybody wins!

Attackers

When your team has the ball, you are an **attacker**. An attacker is either a **forward** or a **midfielder**.

A forward is also called a **striker**. A striker's job is to score goals. Strikers need to be fast runners and good dribblers. Strikers pass back and forth constantly. When a clear shot opens up, the striker tries to score.

Midfielders stay back in the middle of the field. They get ready to defend if the other team steals the ball. They dribble and pass the ball back to the strikers if it bounces their way.

Defenders

When your team doesn't have the ball, then you are a **defender**. Defenders try to get the ball away from the other team. They try to stop the other team from scoring.

Remember: No hands! You can't grab, and you can't shove. Press in close to try to steal away a dribble. Stay on your toes to steal a pass. Crowd the goal to stop a shot. Get in the other team's way and break up the action.

Practice

At practice, your coach will teach you drills to build your skills. You will learn to dribble at top speed without tripping when you switch direction. You will learn to make quick passes that hit their mark.

You will run, run, *run* so that you can go faster, farther, longer.

You will learn the rules of soccer and get set to play.

Game Day

Here are some Game Day tips:

1. Make sure you have what you need *before* it is time to go. If this is hard for you, then make a checklist: jersey, shorts, shin guards, socks, cleats, and a water bottle.

2. Get your gear together the night before a game so you will be set to jet. Maybe have a special soccer bag that can hold all of your stuff.

3. Arrive on time and ready to play.

4. Listen for the whistle! Refs will help you follow the rules. Coaches will make sure everyone gets time to play.

5. Keep your eyes on the action, whether you are on the pitch or on the bench.

6. If you're not in the game, cheer for your teammates.

7. Play hard but have fun. Good sports always have a good time, no matter who wins.

8. High fives all around! Congratulate the players on both teams.

9. Thank the coaches on both teams and the referees.

10. Thank the person who brings the oranges for the halftime snack.

Soccer is a great game. You will learn snappy skills. You will get fresh air and exercise. You will make new friends. Soccer connects you to other kids all around the world. Millions of kids get a kick out of soccer, and you will, too!

A Note to Your Biggest Fan

Parents and caregivers can play a key role in helping kids who are dribbling up the pitch for the first time.

Model model behavior. Teamwork and sportsmanship are critical to any game. Provide encouragement and support to your child, to your child's team, and to your child's opponents. Show respect to the coach, the refs, and other volunteers.

Let the coach coach. You have a couple of jobs to do, but coaching isn't one of them. Be sure your child is on time and ready to play, then take a seat and take it easy.

Away from the field, ask the coach to provide practice tips that will support the team methods and message, and privately discuss any concerns you have about your child's playing time or performance.

Temper your temper. As in any sport, losing is part of the game. Missteps and missed calls can be frustrating for everybody. Keep your cool! The point of soccer at this level is for your child to learn game strategies, get fresh air and exercise, play with friends, and have fun. Developing skills at a natural pace will help your child become a happier, more confident player.